THE
WILSON
READING
SYSTEM

STUDENT
READER
ELEVEN

The Reading Program
(408) 262-1349

by Barbara A. Wilson

SECOND EDITION

Wilson Language Training
162 West Main Street
Millbury, Massachusetts 01527-1943
(508) 865-5699

ISBN 1-56778-022-9 8.00 Student Reader Eleven Item# SR11

ISBN 1-56778-011-3 33.00 Student Readers 7-12 Item# WRS712

ISBN 1-56778-009-1 78.00 Student Readers 1-12 Item# WRS112

ISBN 1-56778-000-8 196.00 WRS Complete Set Item# WRS101

The Wilson Reading System is published by:

Wilson Language Training
162 West Main Street
Millbury, MA 01527-1943

Printed in the U.S.A.

S T E P

11

Concepts

isn't	hasn't	haven't
didn't	hadn't	can't
doesn't	wasn't	weren't
wouldn't	shouldn't	couldn't
aren't	don't	won't

---

he's	she's	it's
that's	who's	what's
there's	here's	let's
you'll	they'll	we'll
he'll	I'll	she'll

---

you've	they've	we've
I've	I'd	she'd
he'd	we'd	they'd
you're	we're	they're
I'm	I've	I'd

---

there's	haven't	she'll
weren't	that's	don't
I've	who's	I'd
couldn't	you're	we'll
won't	we're	aren't

---

1. The delivery didn't arrive in time.

2. Ben can't participate in the game this afternoon.

3. The directions from the manager weren't very clear.

4. Jeff wouldn't give his sister a dime!

5. Ed really shouldn't consume any more food today.

6. Hasn't the weather been perfectly delightful?

7. Mr. Cowler won't attend the conference due to lack of funds.

8. Pam and Dick haven't been able to reach an agreement yet.

9. Lou doesn't want to miss autumn in New England again.

10. Aren't the red, orange and yellow leaves gorgeous?

1. There's a jazz concert on the public television station at eight p.m.

2. Who's pitching in tonight's baseball play-off game?

3. That's where Cathy and Bert had their wedding reception.

4. Let's plan a family camping trip for next spring.

5. Cara is a good basketball player; in fact, she's the best!

6. Ben announced that he's running for selectman in the town election.

7. It's been three years since the renovation project began, and it still hasn't been completed.

8. What's the calculated cost of the new equipment?

9. There's no excuse for Jane's rude comment.

10. James said that he's been able to locate the missing jewels.

1. I've allowed the children to go to the amusement park for the day.

2. They've been gone for several hours now.

3. I'll be able to go to Florida during my vacation.

4. Soon we'll relinquish the power to the next board of directors.

5. We've seen quite a growth in Massachusett's economy.

6. She'll be waiting for the perfect man forever!

7. You've given so much time to that organization.

8. I think that you'll be seated next to my great - uncle.

9. We've attended original productions of that kind in New York.

10. He'll be performing the opening act in Atlanta.

1. Cindy said that you're the best football player in the state!

2. I think we'd better return these overdue books soon.

3. I'm quite pleased with the outcome of the town election.

4. We're getting the Dodge truck since we now need two vehicles.

5. I'd love to travel throughout America and assist many needy people.

6. He'd like to go to college, but it's so expensive!

7. They're in the mood for a repeat match.

8. You're in Yankee territory when you cross into that state.

9. I'm sure they'd contribute to this important cause.

10. Cara said she'd enjoy the concert at Great Woods.

Mary and Dennis

Mary hasn't seen her husband, Dennis, in two weeks. She misses him terribly! He's away for a conference and won't return for yet another week. Mary wasn't able to afford time off to go with him. She's in school and couldn't break until summertime. This doesn't happen often, and Mary's* glad of that! She'll be much more content when Dennis returns. She's been spoiled by his constant company and feels lonely now without him.

*Mary's = Mary is

A Gorgeous Time of Year

It's fall in New England! It's the favorite time of year for many people in that region. The trees paint the land in a gorgeous array of colors. They're red, yellow, orange, peach, cranberry, and golden brown.

Many travelers make their way to this part of the nation during autumn. It doesn't matter which Northeastern state they visit, people are pleased by the wonders around them. They're rarely disappointed by this season.

If you're lucky enough to be in New England in October, you'll be treated to a heavenly sight.

gym	gyp	cyst
myth	system	syllabus
crystal	cymbal	gymnastic
symbolic	symptom	symphonist
Lynn	hymnist	lymph

---

mystic	syndrome	synopsis
lynx	physics	synthetic
syntax	cystic	systematic
syllable	lynch	Flynn
sympathetic	symphony	analytic

---

byte	Kyle	type
style	pyre	Hyde
lyre	syne	hype
Lyle	analyze	electrolyte
megabyte	neophyte	electrolyze

enzyme	typeset	hydrophyte
gypsymoth	sympathy	gypsum
pyx	sync	syndicate
bye	wye	superhype
dye	rye	lye

hyphen	styrofoam	commodity
onyx	cypress	dynamic
hydrogen	agency	cyclone
symphony	gypsy	dynamite
regency	hype	city

---

cycle	gypsum	Kyle
tendency	cynic	astrology
cyanide	geology	mystic
lynch	hydrant	contingency
gymnastic	ancestry	gyrostat

---

synt	metony	gyllope
prodyme	styme	cymote
stymest	crothy	plotryne
crytley	blyst	slemy
mintly	tymirt	shymp

---

phyllon	shymote	croby
spyle	syntem	cyment
trymote	spyle	pryst
closhy	chontly	flymelt
flyst	systop	stype

---

1. When Ben finished at the gym, he was famished!

2. I think you have the symptoms of the bad flu.

3. I do not wish to study physics, but it is a requirement.

4. Gram stitched a dress made of a synthetic cloth.

5. Mr. and Mrs. Babbit were quite excited about their visit to Symphony Hall.

6. Mrs. Flynn stressed the difficulty of the task, but it did not intimidate Tom.

7. Ed wished to develop a more systematic method for billing clients.

8. Mom was quite sympathetic when I told her my problem.

9. Ken could not miss his gymnastics class.

10. At times, Wendy wished that her husband was not so analytic.

1. Tom is such a cynic, he will probably think we're doing this for profit.

2. The author has a syndicated column which appears in the daily newspaper.

3. We'll analyze the report and make our decision over the weekend.

4. The little baby seems to have the flu symptoms.

5. Typesetting is quite an involved task.

6. To read a difficult word, it is helpful to divide it into syllables.

7. Kyle hopes to take a gymnastic class this spring.

8. The crystal lamp is a wedding gift from my husband's family.

9. My analytic approach is desired by my boss.

10. Our company recently procured a two-megabyte hard disk for the computer.

1. Steve had lots of difficulty in his biology class.

2. Jane expressed herself with her style of dress.

3. Kyle went to the agency and had them type his syllabus.

4. The city of Memphis must carefully analyze its spending.

5. Mrs. Halpin was the gypsy who witnessed the crime.

6. Lynn has a tendency to be fickle when it comes to men.

7. Mr. Hyde distracted the hymnist while she sang her solo.

8. I think it would be fun to trace the family ancestry.

9. Jane developed a cyst on her back and had to go to the clinic in the city.

10. Tom would like to study geology, but Lynn would like to study physics.

Exercise for Health

Donna Flynn went to the gym at least three times a week. She realized how important exercise was to her health. Ms. Flynn had a system that she followed. First, she would stretch out. Next, she pedaled several miles on a bicycle at the gym. Donna then swam ten freestyle laps in the Olympic-size pool. She felt extremely refreshed when she finished! This young woman had the type of commitment needed to maintain her shape.

Americans have been into a "health kick" over the past decade. They have been more aware of the need to stay fit. People analyze their food intake more carefully and try to exercise. Donna sets a good example. It's vital to one's health to develop a positive exercise program in today's comfortable world!

ent	ence	ous
al	ible	ate
ity	ism	ant
ance	ery	ory
age	ist	ic

---

ery	ize	ic
ance	ist	age
ory	ism	ible
ary	al	ous
ent	ence	ity

---

cancerous	joyous	continuous
murderous	thunderous	dangerous
ponderous	carbonous	prosperous
marvelous	pompous	famous
hazardous	treasonous	rigorous

_____

accidental	agnostical	festival
intentional	arrival	optional
sectional	professional	nautical
original	fanatical	astrological
institutional	ornamental	sensational

_____

democratic	organic	graphic
alphabetic	acrobatic	alcoholic
classic	diplomatic	poetic
automatic	magnetic	demonic
microscopic	Arabic	cubic

___

ity, ist, ize

purity	activist	vaporize
realize	sparsity	extremist
novelist	loyalist	revolutionize
immensity	rarity	isolationist
victimize	magnetize	minority

___

convincible   destructible   digestible

producible   enforcible   reducible

sensible   resistible   convertible

forcible   connectible   responsible

collapsible   accessible   corruptible

_____

absenteeism   communism   romanticism

organism   absolutism   criticism

extremism   mysticism   fundamentalism

magnetism   collectivism   cynicism

alcoholism   occultism   fanaticism

_____

existent	despondence	consistent
adherence	conference	persistent
occurrence	different	insistence
inference	respondent	coherent
indulgence	existence	correspondence

acquaintance	resistance	descendant
inhabitant	accountant	ignorance
performance	acceptance	attendance
accordance	inheritance	admittance
defendant	assistance	attendant

dictionary	supplementary	bindery
documentary	accessory	shrubbery
slavery	trickery	commentary
migratory	boundary	summary
refinery	crockery	sensory

baggage	yardage	orphanage
considerate	storage	compassionate
coinage	passage	pilgrimage
package	postage	temperate
dosage	proportionate	breakage

contradictory	desirous	footage
arsonist	irresistible	modernize
governmental	expansionism	visionary
legendary	ignorant	consistence
appearance	insistent	nervous

---

rancorous	indulgence	stationery
betrayal	annoyance	considerate
urgent	stationary	triumphant
bribery	mileage	collectible
absurdity	artistic	nutritionist

---

consistency	idealistic	professionalism
classicism	brutally	fanatically
communalism	realistic	forcibly
absorbency	emotionalize	fatalistic
originally	alphabetical	functionally

---

urgency	acrobatically	magnetically
capitalistic	realistically	automatically
emergency	electronically	classically
intentionally	idealistically	alphabetically
authorizing	diplomatically	demonically

11.3

1. The thunderous applause at the end of Act I demonstrated the crowd's praise.

2. The pompous king came to power in the late eighteenth century.

3. The prosperous state is a good example of the man's policies.

4. The actor became famous after his most recent film.

5. Americans must regulate the disposal of hazardous waste.

6. The joyous occasion will be celebrated on November tenth.

7. I think Fred has been a marvelous addition to the staff.

8. The continuous music in the park has been quite pleasant!

9. The rigorous exercise has exhausted me.

10. Jim felt murderous when he was told the bad news.

1. James had an accidental fall on the steep incline.

2. The ornamental hall looks quite festive for the holiday.

3. The hotel will offer an optional, extended vacation plan.

4. The institutional food is really not bad at all.

5. Cathy and Bert plan to go to the big festival held in New Hampshire each spring.

6. The original painting was auctioned for two thousand dollars.

7. Ed has a rational mind yet I do not understand this report!

8. Steve would like to become a professional fighter, but it is unlikely.

9. Jan is hoping to get a sectional couch for the living room.

10. The nautical equipment is very costly.

1. During the Revolutionary War, that family's ancestors were loyalists.

2. James has such a poetic style of writing!

3. We'll hopefully revolutionize that company's inventory organization.

4. Janet would like to be a novelist, and she has the talent to succeed.

5. The democratic system will be used to elect a new club president.

6. We must not allow the greedy people to victimize the helpless.

7. The Arabic community is located on the west side of the city.

8. Bert has a very diplomatic way of making his feelings public.

9. The sparsity of trees in this location indicates that we are near the top.

10. The extremists are in the minority.

1. When Ed pours on his charm, he is irresistible!

2. Paula's absenteeism is not a very sensible way to pass.

3. Alcoholism is on the rise in our country today.

4. It is important to establish enforcible rules in the schools.

5. Alice gave a convincible argument, but Jane still didn't change her mind.

6. The teacher attempted to find out who was responsible for the classroom mess.

7. My idealism remains even though I have seen many negative things.

8. The tent is collapsible and fits into this small pouch.

9. Look into the microscope and see the many organisms on the slide.

10. Those seats are not accessible to the general public.

1. We can't wait to attend the conference in November.

2. There's only one kind of fish in this huge tank.

3. The entire family plans to go to the opening performance.

4. I hope we can find a good accountant to sort out this mess.

5. The poor and homeless in this nation need our assistance.

6. That is quite an indulgent dessert!

7. You've established the fact that the policy was non-existent at the time.

8. The president of the class made an inspirational acceptance speech.

9. I think that statement was quite ignorant.

10. The defendant was insistent about his innocence.

1. The supplementary program will be offered next fall.

2. The cops stopped the chase at the city's boundary.

3. Trickery is rampant on Halloween.

4. The teacher wants a summary paragraph handed in by Friday.

5. The commentary on the debate was more interesting than the debate itself!

6. It is impossible to understand the position favoring slavery.

7. The migratory birds will soon be heading south.

8. The shrubbery along the side of the house needs trimming.

9. I felt a sensory overload with so much happening altogether.

10. Steve will get Kerry that accessory for her wardrobe.

1. Dad is always considerate of Mom's feelings.

2. The package quickly arrived to our satisfaction.

3. The postage for the package is much too expensive.

4. A disproportionate amount of taxes goes to that cause.

5. An orphanage for black children was started by William Still.

6. A high dosage of medication is needed for my pain.

7. Todd ran the football effectively for a yardage gain of ten.

8. We must avoid an energy shortage and conserve whenever possible.

9. Janet has passionate trust in the ability of man.

10. The passage to the city was blocked by the destruction of the bridge.

1. When Cathy and Bert had their baby, it was a joyous occasion.

2. Maureen drives through town in the red convertible that her husband refurbished.

3. Classical music sounds marvelous at a live concert.

4. Tonight there is a television documentary on civil rights.

5. Speeding down the highway is quite dangerous.

6. Sid accidentally dropped his glass of wine on the carpet.

7. My uncle likes to describe the legendary event.

8. The army demands a rigorous training effort.

9. Jim's annoyance with the clerk was very evident.

10. I wish that humorous conversation was recorded.

1. Ed has a very magnetic personality.

2. Barb passionately addressed the state of education.

3. Consistency is so important when raising children.

4. Realistically, the program can't possibly be completed by its deadline.

5. Kevin intentionally walked the baserunner.

6. Jane is emotionally involved with the homeless child.

7. Peg and Jim artistically decorated their new apartment.

8. Dennis was originally going to New York, but he was able to cancel the trip.

9. That puppy is irresistibly cute!

10. Cara accidentally spilled coffee on the living room rug.

Accomplishment

often
discipline
working
anxiety
toward
Kierkegaard

People often think others who meet with success must have more brains and luck than themselves. This is usually not true. What they may have instead is more self-discipline and the ability to make choices.

Success starts with choices. A person decides to pursue something. At this point, it must be realized that in selecting one goal, other goals must be left behind. For example, if a person states as a goal the completion of a woodworking project by a particular date, he or she is also choosing to give up other things. Saturdays must be spent on the project instead of visiting friends or doing errands. There is just not enough time to pursue all endeavors at once!

A feeling of anxiety must be overcome to make most choices that will move a person toward self-development. A person may wish to do the wood project but feel that he or she can't do it properly. This emotion can be expected whenever a choice is made to do something new and different.

Kierkegaard, a Danish philosopher, said that anxiety always arises when a person confronts the possibility of self-development. It is important to recognize this. When a goal is not chosen because of anxiety, a person will often feel depressed. Anxiety is normal with each new goal.

continued

11.3

Accomplishment (continued)

Perseverance is the next challenge! Gratification is not instant. A person may say, "I just can't get motivated to start!" This does not happen automatically– the wood may sit in a pile. A feeling of gratification will not occur for sometime. Motivation does not "kick-in" until the end is in sight. At that point, when a person can start to feel a sense of satisfaction, she becomes highly motivated. That means that the project must be started without motivation! Persistence must occur to drive a project continuously, often slowly, forward.

Success is not accidental. When people make a choice for self-development, despite the nervousness it produces, they have begun. In making the choice, other things must be relinquished. The first labors toward the goal must be started almost without motivation. As persistent action continues, motivation develops, and a goal will be met. The sense of accomplishment is grand, and a person then gains a step in the fulfillment of self-potential.

National Parks

America <u>is</u> beautiful. There are thousands of sensational sights across the nation. Many of these are preserved within the boundary of a national park. The wilderness is under governmental protection in geographical locations throughout the U.S.A. The national park system also manages valued historical monuments, famous battlegrounds, and scenic trails.

The national parks, for the most part, have been lovingly maintained. Seasonal attractions lure people for recreation and enjoyment. Those visiting the parks realize their responsibility to respect its beauty. However, 300 million people per year flood into the system. Conservation of the land, with all its glory, is a must. The national park system is a generous gift to every U.S. citizen. The people, in turn, must show thanks with a strong dedication to keep these parks in their original form.

employing	payment	graying
delayed	convoys	boyhood
joyful	trayful	trolleys
kidneys	straying	stayed
playful	surreying	destroying

---

employment	praying	tomboys
dismayed	volleying	portraying
monkeying	joyous	valleys
annoyed	swayed	enjoyable
wayward	decaying	jerseys

---

glorious	silliest	smellier
carried	married	soggiest
magnified	tallied	applied
plentiful	sloppily	fried
harmonious	frostiest	happier

---

replied	implied	messiest
dirtiest	niftiest	tanginess
dressier	dried	carrier
happily	nastier	sloppiness
luckiest	pestiness	copier

11.4

pennies	agencies	navies
pansies	babies	families
territories	berries	candies
liberties	ladies	copies
factories	sixties	studies

---

cities	flies	flurries
spies	puppies	marries
forties	parties	rallies
hurries	cries	tries
studies	tallies	entries

---

studying	carrying	babying
tallying	implying	worrying
trying	copying	hurrying
tarrying	supplying	ferrying
frying	gratifying	replying

---

marrying	magnifying	crying
drying	fiftyish	applying
rallying	relying	defying
babyish	scurrying	caddying
identifying	emptying	prying

---

delaying	ladies	babyish
stormiest	enemies	hurrying
replying	graying	loveliest
copying	repayable	copied
counties	enjoyable	drier

---

glorious	greediness	flying
laziest	victorious	cries
reliable	player	industrious
turkeys	delayed	ponies
hobbies	galleys	luxurious

---

plineys	bersier	conboyable
stoying	droftiest	blavies
regnified	prolayable	carniness
sterried	stomeyed	flerries
ploggiest	blessied	stolleying

---

plocayed	streyed	robeyment
plastier	stoyful	shallying
stomying	streniment	libneying
survoyed	flubies	stobbies
gloftier	proflayed	clobier

---

1. The trayful of candy will be passed around the room.

2. Hopefully, unemployment will continue to decline in the nation.

3. The birthday party was a joyous occasion.

4. The telephone payment is due this Tuesday.

5. Paul's boyhood was quite enjoyable while he lived along the seashore.

6. The hurricane winds destroyed much property along the eastern coast.

7. Audrey's flight to Vancouver will be delayed for three hours.

8. Dad was annoyed when he could not find his hammer.

9. Barney Bear is such a playful puppy!

10. Many people are praying for peace in the world.

1. Jenny decided to make the silliest costume possible.

2. James fried the shrimp after dipping it in batter.

3. The company will be renting a copier soon.

4. I will happily contribute to the preparation of the feast.

5. Roy married a girl that he met in Germany.

6. Jim has the messiest desk I have ever seen!

7. The picnic was held on a glorious day in late spring.

8. Jane bundled her children in winter coats on the frostiest morning yet.

9. Barb is the happiest lady since she married her husband, Ed.

10. The U.S. carrier will be stationed in the harbor over the weekend.

11.4

1. I saved my pennies for this rainy day trip.

2. Americans should be thankful for their many liberties.

3. The ladies and gentlemen will gather in the hall for the grand presentation.

4. Hopefully, more people in the cities and towns across the nation will soon be reading.

5. The cries of the homeless people must be heard.

6. The factories in this city are shutting down, and many people are unemployed.

7. The garden is bright with red, yellow and pink pansies.

8. Flurries are expected in the Northeast this evening.

9. Cara tries hard to do well in her studies.

10. Ted passed away in his late sixties due to lung cancer.

1. Paula has been trying to get that job for the last ten weeks.

2. Replying to the letter, Steve angrily mailed his response.

3. The scurrying chipmunk collected nuts to last throughout the winter.

4. Peg had to take a break from studying so she went to the campus party.

5. I think Phil will make quite a bit of cash by caddying at the local golf club.

6. There is no need for worrying about the algebra quiz – it will not be difficult.

7. Ed is tallying the score, but I have a feeling I am victorious.

8. Mom is hurrying supper by frying the fish.

9. The outrageous rallying continued throughout the night.

10. The stout man helped by emptying the heavy trash cans.

1. The boys played in the park all afternoon.

2. I had an enjoyable time when Jim and Peg were married.

3. Our company plans to install a new copying system.

4. Our boss felt quite dismayed when he was given the latest sales report.

5. The food is plentiful so I truly hope you can join us.

6. Jane seems happier now than I can ever remember.

7. I think Jake and Steve have the dirtiest jerseys on the team!

8. Mom plans to stop carrying her credit card.

9. Dad has applied for the sales job that will cover a wide territory.

10. We are flying to Alabama, but our flight has been delayed.

Desert Sensation

Most people think the desert holds little color. People picture miles of sand with occasional rocky ledges and cactus plants. However, these hot, arrid places are capable of exploding with various hues. This is infrequent, but quite glorious when it happens!

The conditions for flowering desert plants are not always ideal. They require an adequate amount of winter drizzle combined with a proper balance between hot and cold springtime temperatures. The otherwise bland desert can be transformed into a sensational sight of harmonious color. Brittlebush may suddenly bloom into a golden carpet. One of the loveliest combinations is an orange poppy surrounded by purple-hued lupine. A cliff can become a colorful sight with a flowering, twisted shrub called a cliffrose.

When the desert displays itself in such glory, it provides a most gratifying glimpse at the marvels contained in all forms of life.

State Fair!

Empty grounds are raised into a bustle of activity. Families begin to arrive from counties across the state. The year-long planning and labor is now visible and demonstrated clearly. A state fair begins!

So much happens in a few days' time. One goal of these events is to promote the industries of the state. This is accomplished in the midst of much enjoyment. There are competitions including horse shows and tractor pulls. Ladies and gents present their kitchen masterpieces. The entries are judged, and blue ribbons are proudly worn. There are exhibitions and many displays. Amusement rides and games attract people of all ages. Music can be heard throughout the fairgrounds.

A state fair, in any state, is truly a joyful event!

portliness	merriment	harmonious
scantiness	envious	healthier
sexiness	scratchiness	ceremonious
victorious	craftiest	daintiness
noisier	sleepiness	jolliest

mini	semidecayed	anti-communist
minibike	antiaircraft	semifixed
minicomputer	antipoverty	semiformal
minicar	antidemocratic	semi-independent
minibus	antislavery	semiconcealed

11.5

mediate	phobia	cardiogram
Orient	trio	obvious
piano	obedient	geranium
radiate	zodiac	consortium
patriotic	condominium	radiator

---

median	remedial	cardiac
radiant	Oriental	enunciate
repudiate	audio	obedience
claustrophobia	comedian	cilia
cranial	fiesta	amphibious

---

affiliate	deviate	mediate
ambiance	Maria	ganglia
calcium	effluvium	alien
radio	radiance	jovial
capriole	equilibrium	Kodiak bear

ambidextrous	antifreeze	illustrious
mediator	cranium	imperious
menial	miniskirt	semiweekly
recipient	scrappiest	antibody
antitrust	semicircle	silkiest

1. That boy can be the nastiest person I know.

2. The event will be dressier than I expected.

3. Mom gave Pete a minibike for his birthday.

4. Tom mentioned that he liked Beth's miniskirt!

5. The semiformal for our school will be on April seventh.

6. Our team has been victorious in its last five games.

7. Stan is envious of his wife's accomplishments.

8. We plan to have semiweekly meetings soon.

9. We need to add antifreeze before the winter arrives.

10. Let's form a semicircle to do this next activity.

1. I would like to visit the Orient someday.

2. Eliizabeth went away for the weekend and stayed at a condominium.

3. Ken developed his claustrophobia long ago.

4. Janet's radiance came through as she gave her presentation to the crowd.

5. Joyce planted geraniums in her garden this year.

6. Cathy has such obedient children.

7. It is so much fun planning for the big fiesta.

8. We will have to replace the radiator in our old van.

9. I lack calcium in my diet and really should drink more milk.

10. Jake's dad told him to turn down the blaring radio.

1. I enjoyed the show about the outer space aliens.

2. Jake is ambidextrous and can hit the baseball right-handed as well as left-handed.

3. Heather regretted her obvious mistake.

4. Steven has had cardiac difficulties for several years.

5. Sue is the craftiest person in this class.

6. Dad seems like he's in quite a jovial mood.

7. I'd like to affiliate myself more closely with that organization.

8. It appears that this case will need to go to mediation.

9. The luxurious condominium is on sale for an outrageous amount!

10. The minicomputer will be a big boost to this office.

Robert E. Lee

Few people are called upon to make as momentous a decision as was Robert E. Lee. As a youth, he learned to make difficult choices. He was the male head-of-the-household at the age of twelve. Yet this could not have prepared him for the decision he would need to make later in his life.

As unrest developed in the country, Abraham Lincoln could see an unavoidable war. Lincoln made an inquiry to Lee– would he command the Union forces? Patriotic Lee, siding with the Union, believed that secession was unconstitutional. In addition, he held an anti-slavery position, freeing his own slaves. Yet he was unwilling to command an army against the South.

Lee was then approached by Confederate leaders. Would he command their army? Lee was a gentle and peace-loving man. He did not use his sword, except for defense. Lee was also a man of strong heritage and devotion. He loved his home state of Virginia. Lee tormented over the decision. In the end, his affection for his homeland weighed his decision to accept. Though Lee was not victorious, he is considered a great general in our American history.

11.5

Post Test Step Eleven

nastier	cardiogram	megabyte
symphonist	compassionate	orphanage
continuously	immensity	descendant
corruptible	won't	accidental
fanaticism	synthetically	claustrophobia

---

shymp	semidrome	prystal
survoyed	incrential	chomically
lissionate	spyle	stopous
stoudary	clobier	libneying
delipant	flomatism	phyllor
